Black Beauty

ANNA SEWELL

Level 2

Retold by John Davage

Series Editors: Andy Hopkins and Jocelyn Potter

Pearson Education Limited
Edinburgh Gate, Harlow,
Essex CM20 2JE, England
and Associated Companies throughout the world.

ISBN: 978-1-4058-4281-5

First published by Penguin Books 2000
This edition published 2008

9

Illustrations by Victor Ambrus

Typeset by Graphicraft Ltd, Hong Kong
Set in 11/14pt Bembo
Printed in China
SWTC/09

Published by Pearson Education Ltd

Contents

		page
Introduction		iv
Chapter 1	My Mother	1
Chapter 2	Lessons	3
Chapter 3	Birtwick Park	4
Chapter 4	I Begin Well	6
Chapter 5	My New Friends	8
Chapter 6	James Howard	9
Chapter 7	The Fire	11
Chapter 8	Little Joe Green	14
Chapter 9	I am Ill	15
Chapter 10	I Move Again	18
Chapter 11	Earls Hall	20
Chapter 12	Ginger is Angry	22
Chapter 13	Reuben Smith	23
Chapter 14	An Accident	24
Chapter 15	A London Cab Horse	27
Chapter 16	Jerry Barker	30
Chapter 17	More Changes	32
Chapter 18	My Last Home	34
Activities		39

Introduction

'Always be good, so people will love you. Always work hard and do your best.'

These were the words of Black Beauty's mother to her son when he was only a young horse. At that time, they lived with Farmer Grey. But when Black Beauty got older, this was sometimes very difficult for him. Not everybody was as kind as Farmer Grey.

Anna Sewell was born in Great Yarmouth, in Norfolk, England, in 1820. She had an accident when she was about fourteen years old. After this she could not walk without help. *Black Beauty* was her only book. She wrote it because she loved horses. It hurt her when somebody was unkind to a horse.

There were no cars or buses in those days. There were trains between the towns and cities. In town or in the country you walked, or used a horse. The horse carried you, or pulled you in a carriage, cart or bus. It brought milk, bread and other things to your house.

There were many thousands of horses at work in Europe, America and other countries. Some worked for good, kind people, but some did not. Often the animals had to pull very heavy things, and they had to work for hours and hours. Anna Sewell knew this, and she wanted to tell other people. So she wrote her book.

She was often ill, and in 1871 a doctor told her mother, 'Anna has only eighteen months now.' Soon after this, Anna started writing her book. She finished it in 1877 and died in 1878, only a year after *Black Beauty* went into the bookshops. But many people were kinder to horses after they read Anna's book.

Chapter 1 My Mother

I don't remember everything about the first months of my life. I remember a big field of green grass with one or two trees in it. On hot days my mother stood under a tree and I drank her milk. That was before I got bigger. Then I started to eat the grass.

There were other young horses in the field. We ran and jumped round and round the field. We fell on our backs in the grass and kicked our legs happily.

When I stopped drinking her milk, my mother went to work every day. Then, in the evening, I told her about my day.

'I'm happy because *you* are happy,' she said. 'But remember – you aren't the same as these other young horses. They are going to be farm horses. They're good horses, but we are different. People know your father, and *my* father was Lord Westland's best horse. When you're older, you'll learn to carry people on your back. Or you'll take them from place to place in their carriages.'

'Is that your work, Mother?' I asked. 'Do you do that for Farmer Grey?'

'Yes,' said my mother. 'Farmer Grey sometimes rides me, and sometimes I pull his carriage. Here he is now.'

Farmer Grey came into the field. He was a good, kind man, and he liked my mother.

'Well, my dear,' he said to her, 'here's something for you.' He gave her some sugar. 'And how is your little son?' He put a hand on my back and gave me some bread. It was very nice.

We couldn't answer him. He put a hand on my mother's back, then he went away.

'He's very kind,' my mother said. 'Always do your work happily. Never bite or kick. Then he'll always be nice to you.'

We ran and jumped round and round the field.

Chapter 2 Lessons

I got older and my coat started to shine. It was black, but I had one white foot, a white star on my face and some white on my back.

When I was a big horse, Mr Gordon came to me. He looked at my eyes, my mouth and my legs.

'Very good,' he said. 'Very good. Now he'll have to learn to work. He'll be a very good horse then.'

What does a horse have to learn?

He learns not to move when a man puts a harness on him. Or when the man puts a bit into his mouth. A bit is a cold, hard thing, and it hurts. You can't move it. It stays in your mouth because the head harness goes over your head, under your mouth and across your nose.

I wasn't happy with the bit in my mouth, but Farmer Grey was a kind man in every other way. I didn't bite or kick. My mother always had a bit in her mouth when she worked. Other horses have bits too, and I knew that. So I didn't move when they put it in. Soon it didn't hurt.

The saddle wasn't as bad as the bit. Horses have to learn to have a saddle, and to carry a man, woman, or child on their backs. They have to walk, or to go a little faster. Or to go very fast.

They put the bit in my mouth and the saddle on my back every day. Then Farmer Grey walked with me round the big field. After that, he gave me some good food and spoke to me. I liked the food and the kind words. I wasn't afraid now of the bit and the saddle.

One day Farmer Grey got on my back and sat there in the saddle. The next day he rode me round the field. It wasn't very nice with a man in the saddle, but I was happy with my kind farmer on my back. He rode me in the field every day after that.

The next bad thing were the shoes for my feet. These, too, were cold and hard. A man put them on me. Farmer Grey went with me, but I was afraid. The man took my feet in his hands. Then he cut away some of the hard foot. It didn't hurt me. I stood on three legs when he did the other foot. Then the man made shoes for my feet.

It didn't hurt when he put them on. But I couldn't move my feet easily. But later I started to like the shoes, and the hard roads didn't hurt my feet.

Next I learned to go in carriage harness. There was a very small saddle, but there was a big collar.

Farmer Grey told me to pull a carriage with my mother. 'You'll learn a lot from her,' he said, when he put the harness on me.

I did learn. She showed me the way to move, and she taught me to listen to the driver.

'But there are good drivers and bad drivers,' she said. 'And there are good people and bad people. Farmer Grey is kind, and he thinks about his horses. But some men are bad, or stupid. Always be good, so people will love you. Always work hard and do your best.'

Chapter 3 Birtwick Park

In May a man came and took me away to Mr Gordon's home at Birtwick Park.

'Be a good horse,' Farmer Grey said to me, 'and work hard.'

I couldn't say anything, so I put my nose in his hand. He put a hand on my back and smiled kindly.

Birtwick Park was big. There was a large house. And there were a lot of stables for horses, and places for many carriages. I went to a stable for four horses.

They gave me some food, and then I looked round. There was a horse near me in the stable. He was small and fat, with a pretty head and happy eyes.

'My name is Merrylegs. I'm very beautiful.'

'Who are you?' I asked.

'My name is Merrylegs,' he said. 'I'm very beautiful. I carry the girls on my back. Everybody loves me. You are living in this stable with me, so you will have to be good now. I hope you don't bite.'

A horse looked at Merrylegs from across the stable. She had a very beautiful red-brown coat, but she had angry eyes. She put her ears back.

'Did I bite you?' she asked angrily.

'No, no!' Merrylegs said quickly.

When the red-brown horse went out to work that afternoon, Merrylegs told me about her.

'Ginger does bite,' he said. 'One day she bit James in the arm and hurt him. Miss Flora and Miss Jessie, Mr Gordon's little girls, are afraid of her. They don't bring me nice food now, because Ginger is here.'

'Why does she bite?' I asked. 'Is she bad?'

'Oh, no! I think she was very unhappy. She says, "Nobody was kind to me before I came here." She'll change here. I'm twelve years old, and I know about life. There isn't a better place for a horse than this, anywhere. John is the best groom in the country and James is the kindest boy. Mr Gordon is a very nice man. Yes, Ginger will change here.'

Chapter 4 I Begin Well

The head groom's name was John Manly. He lived with his wife and one little child in a very small house near the stables.

The next morning he took me outside the stable and groomed me. He worked hard, and he made my coat clean and beautiful. Then Mr Gordon came and looked at me.

'He looks very good,' he said. 'I wanted to try him this morning, but I have some other work. You ride him, John, and then tell me about him.'

John put a saddle on my back, but it was too small. He changed it. He got another saddle, not too big and not too small, and we went out. He was a very good rider and I understood his words. On the road we walked, then we went faster. I wanted him to like riding me. Then he took me away from the road to some open fields with one or two trees and a lot of grass. There he wanted me to go very fast, and I did. It was good – I liked it! I think John liked it, too.

When we were at Birtwick Park again, Mr Gordon asked John Manly, 'Well, John, how does he go?'

'He's very good – very good,' said John. 'He loves going fast. He understands you. Nobody was unkind to him when he was young. So he isn't afraid of anybody or anything.'

'Good,' Mr Gordon said. 'I'll ride him tomorrow.'

◆

The next day, John groomed me and put the saddle on me. Then he took me from the stables to the house.

I remembered my mother's words and I tried to make Mr Gordon happy with me. He was a very good rider, and he was kind to me.

His wife was at the door of the big house when he finished riding. 'Well, my dear,' she said, 'how do you like him?'

'He's black and very beautiful,' said Mr Gordon. 'What can we call him?'

'We can call him Black Beauty!' said his wife.

'Black Beauty – yes – yes,' said Mr Gordon. 'I think that's a very good name.'

John came and took me to the stables.

'We've got a name for him, John,' said Mr Gordon. 'My wife thought of it. He's going to be Black Beauty.'

John was very happy. 'Come with me, my Black Beauty,' he said. 'You *are* a beauty – and it's a good English name.'

Chapter 5 My New Friends

John liked me. He was a very good groom, and my black coat always shone beautifully. He looked at my feet every day. He knew when one of them hurt. Then he put something on to it. He often talked to me. I didn't know every word, but I soon understood him. I liked John Manly more than anybody.

I liked the stable boy, James Howard, too. John taught him to be kind to horses, and he helped John to groom me.

After two or three days, I pulled a carriage with Ginger. I was afraid of her. She put her ears back when they took me across to her. But she didn't move when they harnessed me next to her.

John drove us, and we worked very well. Ginger worked well. She pulled as hard as me, and she also liked going more quickly. Many horses only go fast when the driver hits them with his whip. Ginger and I went fast when the driver wanted us to go fast. We went as fast as we could. John didn't like the whip, and he never whipped us. We worked hard for him.

After Ginger and I went out two or three times with the carriage, we were good friends.

We liked little Merrylegs very much. He was never afraid and always happy. Mr Gordon's little girls loved riding him, and they were never afraid. Mrs Gordon loved all three of us, and we loved her.

Mr Gordon liked his people to have one day without work every week. His horses also had a day without work. On Sunday they took us to a field of good grass, and we stayed there all day, without reins or harness. We ran and jumped. We played, and we were happy. Then we stood under some trees and told stories.

Chapter 6 James Howard

Mr Gordon came to the stables one day and spoke to John Manly. 'How is James working, John?' he asked.

'Very well,' John answered. 'He learns quickly. He is kind to the horses, and the horses like him. He's learning to drive, and he'll soon be a good driver.'

Then James came in. 'James,' Mr Gordon said. 'I have a letter from my friend, Sir Clifford Williams of Clifford Hall. He wants to find a good young groom. He pays well, and the young man will soon be head groom. He will have a room, stable clothes and driving clothes, and boys will help him. I don't want to lose you, and John will be sad.'

'I will. Yes, I will,' John said. 'But I won't try to stop him.'

'Yes, we'll all be sad,' Mr Gordon said. 'But we want you to do well, James. Do you want to go? Speak to your mother at dinner-time, James, and then give me your answer. Then I can tell Sir Clifford.'

Ginger and Merrylegs and I were sad, too, when we heard James's answer. He wanted to go. But it was a better job for him. We knew that.

For six weeks before James went, we worked hard. He wanted to be a very good driver, and Mr Gordon and John Manly wanted to help him.

So the carriage went out every day. Ginger and I pulled it, and James drove. James learnt very quickly. For the first three weeks John sat next to him, but after that James drove without him.

One day in autumn, after two or three days of heavy rain, Mr Gordon wanted John to take him to the city. There was a strong wind that day.

We came to the river. The water was very high under the bridge, and there was water across the fields.

We arrived without a problem. But it was late in the afternoon before we started for home again.

The wind was stronger now, and it made a noise in the trees. Suddenly, one of the trees fell across the road with a CRASH!

I was afraid, but I didn't run away. John jumped out of the carriage and came to me.

'We can't go past the tree,' John said to Mr Gordon. 'We'll have to go on the other road to the bridge. It's a longer road and we'll be late. But the horse isn't tired.'

It was nearly dark when we arrived at the bridge. We could see water on it. This sometimes happened when the river was high.

I started to walk across the bridge – but I stopped. Something was wrong. I could feel it.

'Move, Beauty!' said Mr Gordon.

I didn't move, and he put the whip across my back.

'Go now!' he said.

But I didn't go.

'There's a problem,' said John. He jumped down from the carriage and tried to move me. 'What's the problem, Beauty?' he asked.

There was a house across the bridge, and a man ran out of the door. 'Stop! Stop!' he shouted. 'The bridge is breaking in the middle. Don't come across it, or you'll fall in the river!'

John looked at me and smiled. 'Thank you, Beauty,' he said.

We went home on a different road. It was late when we got home. Mrs Gordon ran out of the house.

'You're late!' she said. 'Did you have an accident?'

'We nearly did,' said her husband. 'But Beauty is cleverer than us!'

◆

'I have to go to the city again,' Mr Gordon often said. And we always went when there were a lot of carriages and riders on the road. People were on their way to the train, or they were on their way home across the bridge after work.

Then one day Mr Gordon said to John Manly, 'Mrs Gordon and I have to go to Oxford tomorrow. We'll have Ginger and Black Beauty with the big carriage, and James will drive us.'

It was a journey of about seventy-five kilometres to Oxford. We went about fifty kilometres in one day and then we stopped for the night at the biggest hotel in Aylesbury. James drove very well. We pulled the carriage up and down, and he always stopped on the way up. He never drove us fast when we went down. We had to go quickly when the road was good, but not on bad roads. These things help a horse. And when he gets kind words, too, he is happy.

They groomed us in the hotel stable, and gave us some good food. James said, 'Good night, my beauties. Sleep well, Ginger. Sleep well, Black Beauty.' Then he went to his bed.

Chapter 7 The Fire

An hour later, a man came to the hotel on a horse. One of the hotel grooms brought the horse to the stable.

At Birtwick Park nobody smoked in the stables, but this man did. There was no food in the stable for the new horse, so the groom went to get some. The food for the horses was on the floor above the stable. The groom went up there and found some food. He threw it on the floor for the horse, and he went away.

I slept, but I soon woke up again. I was very unhappy. But why? I didn't know.

I heard Ginger. She was unhappy, too.

Then I saw the smoke.

Very soon there was smoke everywhere. There were noises from above my head – the sounds of a fire. The other horses in the stable woke up. They moved their feet and tried to get away from the smoke.

I was very afraid.

Then the hotel groom came into the stable and tried to take the horses out. But he was afraid, too, and he tried to work quickly. That made us more afraid, and the other horses didn't want to go with him. When he came to me, he tried to pull me out fast. He pulled and pulled. I couldn't go with him.

We were stupid – yes! But we didn't know him, and he was very afraid.

There was more and more smoke. And then we saw the red light of fire from the floor above our heads. Somebody shouted 'Fire!' outside, and more men came into the stable.

The sound of the fire was louder and louder. And then – James was at my head. He spoke to me quietly: 'Come, my beauty. We have to go now. Wake up and come with me. We'll soon get out of this smoke.'

He put a coat round my head and over my eyes. Then I couldn't see the fire, and I wasn't afraid. He spoke to me kindly and we walked out of the stable.

'Here, somebody,' James called. 'Take this horse, and I'll go back for the other horse.'

A big man took me, and James ran into the stable again. I was very unhappy when I saw him do this. I made a lot of noise. (Next day, Ginger said, 'When I heard you, I wasn't afraid. So I came out with James.')

A lot of things happened all round me, but I watched the stable door. There was fire and smoke inside, and things fell to the ground.

Mr Gordon ran to the stable. 'James! James Howard!' he called. 'Are you there?' There was no answer, but I heard more noises in the stable. Other things fell from the top floor. I was very afraid for James and Ginger.

I was happy when James and Ginger came out through the smoke to us.

He spoke to me kindly and we walked out of the stable.

'Good boy!' Mr Gordon said to James. 'Are you all right?'

James couldn't speak because of the smoke, but he was fine. He put a hand on Ginger's head and looked happy.

Chapter 8 Little Joe Green

James and Ginger were ill the next day. The smoke was bad for them. So we stayed in Aylesbury for that day. But after another night there, they were better. In the morning we went to Oxford.

James did everything for Ginger. He spoke to older grooms and they told him the best ways. When we arrived home at Birtwick Park, we were all fine.

John heard James Howard's story, and he looked at Ginger and me.

'You did well, James,' he said. 'A lot of people can't get horses out of a stable when there's a fire. Why don't they want to move? Nobody knows. Only a friend can take them out. They have to know and love him.'

Before he left us for his new job, James asked, 'Who's going to do my job? Do you know?'

'Yes,' John said. 'Little Joe Green.'

'Little Joe Green!' said James. 'He's only a child!'

'He's fourteen,' John said.

'But he's very small,' said James.

'Yes, he's small, but he's quick,' said John. 'And he wants to learn, and he's kind. His father will be happy, and Mr Gordon wants to have him here.'

James wasn't very happy about it. 'He's a good boy,' he said. 'But you'll have a lot of work because he's small.'

'Well,' John said, 'work and I are good friends. I'm not afraid of work.'

‘I know that,’ said James. ‘And I’ll try hard to be the same.’

The next day, Joe came to the stables. James wanted to teach him before he went. James learnt to clean the stable, and to bring in our food. He cleaned the harnesses, and helped to wash the carriages. He couldn’t groom Ginger or me because he was too small. So James helped him groom Merrylegs.

Merrylegs wasn’t very happy. ‘The boy knows nothing,’ he said. But after a week or two he said, ‘I think the boy will be good. I’ll help him to learn quickly.’

Little Joe Green was a happy boy. He sang when he worked. We soon liked him.

Chapter 9 I am Ill

One night, after James went away, I heard John outside. He ran to the house, then he ran to the stable. He opened the door and came to me.

‘Wake up, Beauty!’ he said. ‘You have to run now!’

He put a saddle on me very quickly, and he jumped on my back. Then he rode me quickly to the house. Mr Gordon was there, with a light in his hand.

‘Now, John,’ he said, ‘you have to ride as fast as you can. My wife is very ill. Give this letter to Doctor White in Hertford. I want him to come quickly. You can come home when Black Beauty is ready for the journey.’

John took the letter, and we went away.

‘Now, Beauty,’ said John. ‘Do your best!’

It was night, but I knew the road. There were no people on it because they were all in bed and asleep. I went very fast – faster than every journey before that night.

When we came to the bridge, John pulled the reins. I went across it more slowly.

'Good, Beauty!' he said.

When we were across it, I went fast again. We went up and down, past fields and houses, and then through the streets of Hertford.

My shoes made a noise on the road when I stopped at the doctor's door. It was three o'clock in the morning. The doctor's window opened, and Doctor White looked out of it.

'What do you want?' he asked.

'Mrs Gordon is very ill,' John told him. 'Mr Gordon wants you to go quickly, or she'll die. Here's a letter from him.'

'I'll come down,' said the doctor. He shut the window and he was soon at the door. He read the letter. 'Yes,' he said, 'I'll have to go. But my old horse was out all day, and he's very tired now. My other horse is ill. What can I do? Can I have your horse?'

'He ran fast on the way here,' John said. 'But I think he can take you.'

'I'll be ready soon,' the doctor said, and he went into the house again.

John stood next to me and put his hand on my head. I was very hot.

The doctor came out in his riding clothes and with a riding whip.

'You won't want a whip,' John said. 'Black Beauty will go as fast as he can.'

'Thank you,' the doctor said. He gave the whip to John and spoke to me: 'Now, Black Beauty!'

The doctor was a bigger man than John, and he wasn't a very good rider. But I ran for him.

I was very tired, but we arrived at Birtwick Park very quickly. Then I nearly fell down. Mr Gordon heard us. He ran to the door and took the doctor into the house.

Little Joe Green was outside the door, and he took me to the stable. I was happy now, but I was very, very hot. My coat was hot, and water ran down my legs.

Joe was young and very small, but he tried. He cleaned my legs and my back, but he didn't put anything over me. He thought, 'The horse is hot and he won't like it.' He brought me a lot of water. It was cold and very nice, and I drank it. Then he gave me some food.

'Now sleep, Beauty,' he said, and he went away.

Soon I started to feel cold and ill. I tried to sleep, but I couldn't.

I was very ill when John came. He walked from Hertford, but he came to me. I was on the floor.

'Oh, Beauty!' he said. 'What did we do to you?'

I couldn't tell him, but he knew. He put things over me and made me warm. Then he ran to his house and brought hot water. He made a good drink for me. He was angry.

I heard him with the other men. 'A stupid boy!' he said. 'A stupid boy! He puts nothing on a hot horse! He gives him cold water! Oh, Beauty!'

I was very ill for a week. John was with me for hours every day, and he came to me two or three times every night. Mr Gordon came every day, too.

'Dear Beauty,' he said one day. 'My good horse! My wife didn't die, and we can thank you for that! Yes, we have to thank you!'

I was very happy about that. We all loved Mrs Gordon. Doctor White came one day when he was at Birtwick Park. He put a hand on my head and told John, 'Mrs Gordon is here today because this beautiful horse brought me here quickly.'

John said to Mr Gordon, 'Black Beauty went very fast that night. Do you think that he knew?'

I did know. John and I had to go fast for dear Mrs Gordon. I knew that very well.

Chapter 10 I Move Again

I was happy at Birtwick Park for another year. Only one thing made us sad: Mrs Gordon got better, but she was often ill again.

Then the doctor said, 'You and your wife have to go away and live in the south of France, Mr Gordon.'

'We'll go,' said Mr Gordon. 'We'll make a new home there.'

We were very sad. Mr Gordon was unhappy, too, but he started to get ready. We heard a lot of talk about it in the stable. John was very sad. Joe nearly stopped singing when he worked.

Mr Gordon's little girls came to the stable. They visited Merrylegs for the last time. They cried, but they told Merrylegs: 'You'll be happy, old friend. Father is giving you to Mr Good, the kind old church man. You'll take his wife from place to place, but you will never work hard. Joe will go with you. He's going to be the groom and he's going to help in their house next to the church. You'll see your friends Black Beauty and Ginger sometimes. Father is selling them to Lord Westland at Earls Hall. That isn't a long way.'

Mr Gordon wanted to find a job for John, too. But John wanted to open a school and teach young horses their work.

'A lot of young horses are afraid when they learn new things,' he said. 'Horses are my friends, and they like me. I think they'll learn better from a kind person. I want to teach them.'

'Nobody can do it better than you, John,' Mr Gordon said. 'Horses love you. And I'm very sad because I won't see you.'

The last day came. Ginger and I took the carriage to the door of the house for the last time. People came to the door when Mr Gordon brought his wife down in his arms. Many people cried when we moved away.

Mr Gordon's little girls visited Merrylegs for the last time.

Chapter 11 Earls Hall

The next morning, Joe came and he took Merrylegs away to Mr and Mrs Good's house.

John rode Ginger and took me to Earls Hall. It was a very big house with a lot of stables.

At the stables, John asked for Mr York, the boss of the drivers and grooms.

Mr York came and looked at us. 'Very good,' he said. 'They look very good, but horses are very different. You and I know that. What can you tell me about these two?'

'Well,' John said, 'there aren't any better horses than these in the country. But they are different. Black Beauty is never angry or afraid because nobody was unkind to him. When she came to us, Ginger was very unhappy. She often bit and kicked people. She changed at Birtwick Park. We were kind to her, and she's very good now. But people will have to be kind to her, or she will be bad again.'

'I'll remember that,' Mr York said. 'But there are a lot of drivers and grooms here. I can't watch all of them.'

Before they went out of the stable, John said, 'I have to tell you something. Not one of our horses at Birtwick Park used a bearing rein.'

'Well, they'll have to have a bearing rein here,' said Mr York.

'Oh,' said John.

'I don't like bearing reins, and Lord Westland is very kind to horses,' said Mr York. 'But Lady Westland – she's different. For her, everything has to look good. Her carriage horses have to have their heads up. So they have to have bearing reins.'

John spoke to us for the last time. Then he went, and we were very sad.

Lord Westland came to us the next day.

'Mr Gordon says they are good horses. I think he's right,' he said. 'But we can't have one black horse and one brown horse in front of a carriage in London. They can pull the carriage here in the country, and in London we can ride them.'

'They didn't have bearing reins at Mr Gordon's,' said Mr York. 'John told me.'

'Well,' Lord Westland said, 'put the bearing reins on, but only pull them up slowly. I'll speak to Lady Westland about it.'

In the afternoon a groom harnessed Ginger and me to a carriage, and then the groom took us to the front of the house. It was very big – bigger than Birtwick Park – but I didn't like it very much.

Lady Westland came out of the house. She was a tall woman. She walked round us and looked at us. She wasn't happy about something, but she didn't say anything. She got into the carriage. York put the whip lightly across my back, and we walked away.

The bearing rein wasn't bad that day. I always walked with my head up, and the rein didn't pull it up higher.

'Will Ginger be angry with the rein?' I thought.

But she was very good.

At the same time the next day we went to the door again.

Lady Westland came out and said: 'York, pull those horses' heads up.'

York got down and said, 'Please don't be angry with me, Lady Westland. These horses didn't use a bearing rein before now, and Lord Westland said, "Pull their heads up slowly." Do you want me to pull them higher now?'

'Yes!' she said.

York came to our heads and made the reins shorter.

When we climbed to higher ground, we wanted to put our heads down. We had to pull harder. The bearing rein stopped us, and our legs and backs had to work harder.

Ginger said to me, 'This isn't too bad. I won't say anything because they are kind to us here in every other way. I don't want to be bad, but bearing reins make me very angry.'

Chapter 12 Ginger is Angry

One day Lady Westland came out in very expensive clothes.

'Drive to Lady Richmond's house,' she said. But she didn't get into the carriage. 'When are you going to get those horses' heads up, York? Pull them up now!'

York came to me first. He pulled my head back with the bearing rein. It hurt me, and the bit cut my mouth.

Then he went to Ginger and he began to pull her head back. Ginger stood up on her back legs. Her ears went back, and her eyes were very angry. She began to kick and she tried to get away from the carriage. York and the groom couldn't stop her. Then she caught her legs in the harness and fell.

York sat on Ginger's head. He told the groom to get a knife and cut the harness. Lady Westland went into the house.

Nobody had time for me. I stood with my head back. The bit hurt my mouth.

Then York came and took away the bearing rein. He said, 'Why do we have to have these bearing reins? They make good horses bad, and they make our work harder. Lord Westland will be angry. But how can I say no to his wife when *he* never does?'

They never put Ginger into carriage harness again at Earls Hall. When she was well again after her fall, one of Lord Westland's younger sons took her for his riding horse.

I worked with the carriage, and for four months the bearing rein hurt me every day. I worked with Max, an older horse. He came from Lord Westland's stable in London.

'Why do they have to hurt us with bearing reins?' I asked him.

'They do things that way in London,' he said. 'In London the rich people's horses have to have their heads up. It made me ill, so I'm here now. I'll die soon.' He looked at me sadly. 'I hope you don't have to have the bearing rein every day. You'll die before you're old, too. People are very stupid.'

Chapter 13 Reuben Smith

In April, Lord and Lady Westland went to their London house and took York with them. Ginger and I and three or four other horses stayed at Earls Hall. Their sons and their sons' friends rode us.

Reuben Smith was the boss of the stables when York was away. He was a very good driver and a good groom. He liked horses, and horses liked him. Why was he only the groom? Why wasn't he a boss, too?

Max told me about him.

Reuben Smith sometimes got drunk. When he wasn't drunk, he was very good at his work. Everybody liked him. But when he was drunk, he wasn't the same man.

'I'll never get drunk again,' he told York. And so York wasn't afraid to leave the horses with Smith when he, York, was away.

◆

One day Lord Westland's younger son wanted to go to London.

'I'll get on the train at Hertford,' he told Smith. 'I want you to drive me there in my carriage. It can stay in the carriage-maker's in Hertford, because I want him to do some work on it. So bring a saddle and ride Black Beauty home to Earls Hall.'

Reuben Smith drove me to the carriage-maker's. Then he put the saddle on me and rode me to the White Horse hotel. There he asked the hotel groom for some good food for me.

'Have him ready for me at four o'clock,' he said.

He went to the hotel, and he met some men at the door. He came out again at five o'clock and told the hotel groom, 'I don't want to go before six. I'm with some old friends.'

The groom showed Smith one of my front shoes. 'That shoe will fall off soon,' he told Smith. 'Do you want me to do something about it?'

'No,' Smith said. 'It can't fall off before we get home.'

Those were strange words. Reuben Smith was usually careful about our shoes.

◆

He didn't come out at six o'clock – or at seven – or at eight. At nine o'clock he came out of the hotel with a lot of noise.

'You!' he shouted to the hotel groom. 'Bring me my horse!'

He was very angry with the groom – with everybody in the hotel. Why? I didn't know.

We weren't out of Hertford when he started to hit me with his whip. I went as fast as I could. He whipped me again.

It was dark, and I couldn't see very well. The road was very hard, and bad in places, and my shoe soon fell off.

But Smith was drunk and didn't see it. He didn't stop. He whipped me and shouted at me.

'Faster! Faster!' he cried.

The bad road cut into the foot without a shoe and hurt me.

And then I fell and threw Smith over my head on to the road. It was an accident.

He didn't move.

My legs hurt, but I stood up. I moved to the grass near the road and waited.

Chapter 14 An Accident

I waited there for a long time.

It was nearly midnight when I heard a horse's feet. Then I saw Max and a cart. They came down the road. I called to Max, and he answered me.

There were two grooms in the cart. They wanted to find Reuben. One of them jumped down from the cart and ran across to the man on the road.

I threw Smith over my head on to the road.

'It's Reuben, and he isn't moving,' he said. 'He – he's dead – cold and dead!'

The other groom got out of the cart and came to me. He used one of the cart's lights and looked at the bad cuts on my legs.

'Black Beauty fell!' he said. 'Black Beauty! What happened?'

He tried to take me to the cart, and I nearly fell again.

'Oh!' he said. 'Black Beauty's foot is bad, too. And look – there's no shoe! Why did Reuben ride a horse without a shoe?' He looked at the other groom, then said, 'He was drunk again!'

They put Reuben Smith into the cart, and then one of the grooms drove it to Earls Hall. The other man put something round my bad foot and we walked on the grass near the road.

The cuts on my legs and my bad foot hurt me, but after some time we got home.

◆

I was ill for weeks after that. The grooms did everything for me, but the cuts were very bad. When I could walk, they put me into a small field. My foot and my legs got better, but only after many weeks.

One day Lord Westland came to the field with York. He looked at my legs and was angry.

'We'll have to sell him,' he said. 'I'm very sad, because my friend Mr Gordon wanted Black Beauty to have a happy home here. But you'll have to send him to Hampstead.'

And so I went to Hampstead. One day each week they sell horses there.

A lot of people came and looked at me. The richer people went away when they saw my legs. Other people looked at my teeth and eyes, and they felt my legs. I had to walk for them. Some people's hands were hard and cold. To them I was only a horse for work. But some had kind hands, and they spoke to me kindly. They learnt more about me than the other people.

I liked one of the kind men. 'I can be happy with him,' I thought. 'He likes horses and he's kind to them.'

He was a small man, but he moved well and quickly, and his hands and his eyes were friendly.

'I'll give twenty-three pounds for this horse,' he said.

'Say twenty-five pounds, Mr Barker, and you can have him,' another man said. He sold the horses – it was his job.

'Twenty-four and no more,' the little man said.

'All right, I'll take twenty-four pounds,' said the other man. 'You've got a very good horse for your money, Jerry Barker. He'll be very good for cab work. You'll be very happy with him.'

The little man paid the money, then he took me away to a hotel. There was a saddle there for me. He gave me some very good food, and soon we were on our way to London.

Chapter 15 A London Cab Horse

There were a lot of horses and carriages and carts in the streets of the great city. It was night, but there were a lot of people on the roads and under the street lights.

There were streets and streets and streets. Then Jerry Barker called to somebody, 'Good night, George.'

Cabs waited in this street.

'Hello, Jerry!' came the answer. 'Have you got a good horse?'

'Yes, I think I have,' said Jerry.

'That's good. Good night.'

Soon we went up a little street, and then into a street with small houses. Opposite the houses there were stables and carriage-houses.

Jerry Barker stopped me at one of the little houses and called, 'Are you asleep?'

The door opened, and a young woman ran out, with a little girl and a boy.

'Hello! Hello! Hello!' they shouted happily.

My rider got down from the saddle.

'Hello!' he said. 'Now, Harry, open the stable door and I'll bring him inside.'

Soon we were all in the little stable. The woman had a light in her hand, and they looked at me.

'Is he good, Father?' asked the little girl.

'Yes, Dolly, as good as you are. Come and put a hand on him.'

The little girl wasn't afraid.

'She's nice, and she's kind,' I thought. 'I'm going to love her.'

'I'll get him some nice food, Jerry,' the woman said.

'Yes, all right, Polly,' said Jerry.

Jerry loved his wife Polly, and his son and daughter. His son, Harry, was twelve years old. His daughter, Dolly, was eight. They loved him, too.

I never knew happier people. They didn't have a lot of money, because people didn't pay cab drivers very well. But they were always kind, and their love came out of the little house to the stable.

Jerry had a cab and two horses. The other horse was a big old white horse called Captain. That night, Captain told me about the work of a London cab horse.

'Only one horse pulls the cab,' he said. 'Mr Barker works for about sixteen hours each day from Monday to Saturday, but you and I will only work for eight hours. It's hard work, but Jerry is never unkind. A lot of cabmen are unkind, but not Jerry. You'll love him.'

And he was right.

Captain went out with the cab in the morning. Harry came into the stable after school and gave me food and water.

When Jerry came home for his dinner, Polly cleaned the cab. Harry helped Jerry to put the harness on me. They did it slowly because they didn't want to hurt me. There was no bearing rein, and the bit didn't hurt.

I was a London cab horse!

'I think he'll be happy with that,' Jerry said.

'What's his name?' Polly asked.

'The man in Hampstead didn't know,' said Jerry. 'We can call him Jack. We called our last horse Jack. What do you think, Polly?'

'Yes, all right,' said his wife. 'It's a good name.'

So Jack was my new name, and I started work.

I was a London cab horse!

Chapter 16 Jerry Barker

We went down the street and Jerry took me to a place behind the other cabs.

A big cabman came to me with other drivers. He was the oldest cabman there. He looked at me and put a hand on my back and legs.

'Yes,' he said, 'he's the best horse for you, Jerry Barker. You paid a lot of money for him, but you did well. He's a good horse, and he'll work hard for you.'

My work was very hard. The great city was a new place for me. I wasn't happy with the noise, the thousands of people, the horses, carriages and carts in the streets. But Jerry was a very good driver, and I wanted to make him happy. We did well.

Jerry never whipped me. Sometimes he put the whip on my back. That meant 'Go!' But he usually only moved the reins when he wanted me to go.

He and Harry groomed us well, and Captain and I always had good food, clean water and a clean stable. Harry was clever with stable work, and Polly and Dolly cleaned the cab in the mornings. They laughed and talked. They were a happy family.

One morning an old cab stopped next to ours. The horse was tired and thin. She was a brown horse and she looked at me with tired eyes.

'Black Beauty!' she said. 'Is it really you?'

'Ginger?' I said.

It *was* Ginger, but a very different Ginger. She told me her story. It was a very sad story.

'After a year at Earls Hall, they sold me,' said Ginger. 'But I was ill again and a horse-doctor came. Then a cabman bought me. He's got a lot of cabs and other cabmen use them. They pay him for them. These men aren't always careful or kind. They whip me and I have to work seven days a week. My life is hard. I'm very tired now. I'll be happy when I die.'

'I'm very sorry, Ginger,' I said.

I put my nose near hers. I think she was happy.

'You were a good friend,' she said.

Some weeks after this, a cart went past us. There was a dead horse in the back. It was a brown horse. I think it was Ginger.

Sometimes a person wanted Jerry to go fast in the cab. Often Jerry said, 'No. You want to go fast because you got up late. You have to start your journey early, and then you can get there more slowly.'

Sometimes people wanted to give him more money, but he did not go faster. But after I learnt to go through the London streets, we could go faster than most cabs.

'We'll go fast when somebody has to get somewhere quickly, Jack,' Jerry said to me.

We knew the quickest roads to the hospitals in London, and sometimes we made very quick journeys to them.

◆

One wet day we took a man to his hotel. After he went inside, a young woman spoke to Jerry. She had a little boy in her arms, and he was very ill.

'Where is St Thomas's Hospital?' she asked. 'Can you tell me? I'm from the country, and I don't know London. The doctor gave me a letter for St Thomas's Hospital. The hospital can help my son.'

'It's a long way, dear,' Jerry said. 'You can't walk there – not in this rain and with the boy in your arms. Get into the cab and I'll take you there.'

'Thank you,' she said, 'but I can't do that. I haven't got any money.'

'Did I say anything about money?' said Jerry. 'I'm a father, and I love children. I'll take you. Please get in.'

He helped her into the cab. She started to cry and he put a hand on her arm. Then he climbed up and took the reins. 'Let's go, Jack,' he said.

At the hospital Jerry helped the young woman through the big front door.

'I hope your little boy will soon be better,' he said.

'Thank you, thank you!' she said. 'You're a good, kind man.'

A woman came out of the hospital. She heard the words and looked at the 'good, kind man'.

'Jerry Barker!' she said. 'Is it you?'

Jerry smiled.

'Good,' the woman said. 'I can't find a cab today, in this weather, and I have to catch a train.'

'I'll take you,' said Jerry. 'Where do you want to go?'

'Paddington Station,' said the woman.

Chapter 17 More Changes

We took the woman to her train. Her name was Mrs Fowler and she knew Polly.

She asked a lot of questions about Polly and the two children. Then she said: 'And how are you, Jerry?'

'I'm all right now, Mrs Fowler,' said Jerry. 'But I was very ill last January. Polly doesn't like me to work in bad weather, but I *have* to work.'

'The cold weather is bad for you, Jerry,' said Mrs Fowler. 'You'll have to find different work. You can't be a cabman now.'

'I'd like to find work in the country,' said Jerry. 'Polly and the children like the country. But there isn't any work for me there.'

Before she caught her train, Mrs Fowler gave Jerry some money for the children.

'People in the country want good grooms and drivers,' she said. 'When you stop cab work, write to me.'

'Thank you,' said Jerry.

Every year Jerry was ill in the winter. But he didn't stop working, and he got iller and iller.

◆

One year, at Christmas, we took two men to a house, and they said to Jerry, 'Come here again at eleven o'clock.'

Jerry arrived at the right time, but the men didn't come out of the house. We waited and waited. It was a very cold night, and it snowed. Jerry put an old coat over me, then he tried to stay warm.

At one o'clock the two men came out of the house and got into the cab. They didn't say 'Sorry, we're late.' They didn't say anything.

When we arrived home, Jerry was ill. He couldn't work the next day, or the next day.

Polly cried about it. 'What can I do?' she said.

Then, one day, a letter came for Polly. It was from Mrs Fowler:

Dear Polly,

My groom is leaving. He is going to do other work, and he wants to go next month. His wife will go with him, and she is my cook. Would you like to work for me? Jerry can be my groom and driver, and Harry can help him. You can be my cook. There is a little house for you.

Please say you will come.

Mary Fowler

Jerry and Polly talked about it for two days. Then Polly wrote an answer. Her letter said, 'Yes, Jerry and I want to work for you, Mrs Fowler.'

I was very happy for them, but I was sad, too. I loved Jerry and Polly and the two children.

Some of Jerry's cabmen friends wanted to have me, but Jerry wanted me to have a better home.

'Jack's getting old,' he said, 'and the work of a cab horse is too hard.'

Before Jerry, Polly and the children went away, Jerry sold me to a farmer. His name was Mr Thoroughgood, and he knew about horses.

'I'll take Jack, your horse,' he said. 'I'll give him the best food and some weeks in a good field. Then I'll find a new home for him – with a good, kind person.'

Mr Thoroughgood took me away. It was April.

Jerry was ill after a bad time in January and February, but he came outside, with Polly and Harry and Dolly. He saw me for the last time.

'You'll be happy, dear old Jack,' Dolly said. 'I'll always remember you.'

Chapter 18 My Last Home

Mr Thoroughgood was very kind to me, and I had a very happy time on his farm.

'I feel younger,' I thought. But I wasn't a young horse now.

One day Mr Thoroughgood told the groom, 'We have to find a good home for Jack. He can work, I think, but not too hard.'

'The women at Rose Hall are looking for a good horse for their small carriage,' said the groom. 'They don't want a young horse. Young horses sometimes go too fast or run away.'

Mr Thoroughgood thought about that. Then he said, 'I'll take Jack to them. He's the horse for them. But will they be afraid when they see his legs? He hurt them somewhere. I'll take him to Rose Hall tomorrow. They can look at him.'

The next morning the groom cleaned my black coat, and then Mr Thoroughgood took me to Rose Hall.

The women were at home, but their driver was away. One of the women, Miss Ellen, liked me when she saw me.

'He has a very good, kind face,' she said. 'We'll soon love him.'

'He's very good,' Mr Thoroughgood said. 'But he fell down. Look at his legs.'

'Oh!' Miss Ellen's older sister said. She was Miss Bloomfield. 'Will he fall again?'

'I don't think he will,' the farmer said. 'He fell because he had a bad driver. Try him, Miss Bloomfield. Send your driver for him tomorrow. He can try Jack for a day or two.'

Miss Bloomfield was happier. 'You always sell us very good horses, Mr Thoroughgood,' she said. 'Thank you. We'll do that.'

The next morning a nice young man came to Mr Thoroughgood's farm. He looked at me and at my legs. Then he asked Mr Thoroughgood, 'Why are you selling this horse? I'm not happy with his legs.'

The farmer answered, 'I won't sell him before you try him. But I think you'll like him. Ride him, and then tell me. Say yes, and you can have him. Say no, and he can come home here.'

The groom took me to Rose Hall.

That evening he began to groom me. When my face was clean, he stopped. He looked at the white star.

'I remember Black Beauty's white star,' he said. 'He was a wonderful horse. And when I look at this horse's head, I remember Black Beauty's head too. Where is Black Beauty now? I'd like to know.'

When he came to my back, he stopped again. 'Here's some white on his back,' he said. 'That's strange. When I look at it, I remember the white on Black Beauty's back!'

The groom stood and looked at me. 'Black Beauty's star! Black Beauty's one white foot! The white on Black Beauty's back! It *is* Black Beauty!' he said. 'You are Black Beauty, my old friend! Beauty! Beauty! Do you know me? I was little Joe Green, and I nearly killed you.'

And he put his arms round my head.

I remembered a small boy, and this was a man. But it was Joe Green, and I was very happy. I put my nose up to him in a friendly way. And I never saw a happier man than him.

'This is wonderful, Beauty,' he said. 'We'll try to make you happy here.'

The next day Joe groomed me again and harnessed me to a very good small carriage. Miss Ellen wanted to try me, and Joe Green went with her. She was a good driver, and she was happy with me. Joe talked to her about me.

'He's Mr Gordon's old Black Beauty!' Joe said, happily. 'He's a wonderful horse!'

When we came back to Rose Hall, Miss Bloomfield came to the door.

'He's a beautiful horse,' she said. 'Is he a good horse, too?'

'Yes,' Miss Ellen said. 'Very, very good. His name is Black Beauty, and he was at Birtwick Park with Mr Gordon. Our dear friend Mrs Gordon loved him.'

'Beauty nearly died when he got the doctor for Mrs Gordon,' said Joe. And he told them the story.

'I'm going to write to Mrs Gordon. I'll tell her about Black Beauty,' said Miss Ellen. 'She'll be very happy.'

The next day they harnessed me to the carriage, and Miss Bloomfield drove in it. She said to Miss Ellen, 'We'll have the horse and we'll use his old name, Black Beauty.'

◆

It is a year later now. Joe is the best and kindest groom, and everybody loves me.

Miss Ellen says, 'We'll never sell you, Beauty.'

So I'll work happily for them. I'm not afraid of anything.

ACTIVITIES

Chapters 1–5

Before you read

1 Look at the Word List at the back of this book, and find new words in your dictionary. What four things do you put on a horse? What three things does a horse pull?

cab saddle reins cart harness carriage bit

2 There are films of *Black Beauty*. Do you know any of them? What do you know of the Black Beauty story? Discuss this with another student. Then read the Introduction to the book.

While you read

3 Which person do we meet first? Write a number, 1–5, after each name.

a Farmer Grey .....
b James Howard .....
c John Manly .....
d Mr Gordon .....
e Mrs Gordon .....

After you read

4 Are these words for Merrylegs or Ginger?

bites small fat red-brown pretty head angry eyes

5 Who says these words?

a 'Always do your work happily. Never bite or kick. Then he'll always be nice to you.'
b 'Now he'll have to learn to work. He'll be a very good horse then.'
c 'You'll learn a lot from her.'
d 'One day she bit James in the arm and hurt him.'
e 'Nobody was unkind to him when he was young.'
f 'We can call him Black Beauty.'

6 Work with another student. Have this conversation.

Student A: You are Mr Gordon. You want to know about your new horse. Ask John Manly about him.

Student B: You are John Manly. Tell Mr Gordon about Black Beauty. How is he different from Merrylegs and Ginger?

Chapters 6–8

Before you read

7 In the next three chapters Black Beauty is afraid, first of water and then of fire. What do you think is going to happen? Talk about this with another student.

While you read

8 Write the best word in each sentence.

carriage coat floor groom harnesses
hotel middle smoke stable water

- **a** Sir Clifford Williams wants a young ....
- **b** Black Beauty and Ginger pull the ....
- **c** The .... in the river is very high.
- **d** The bridge is breaking in the ....
- **e** They stop at a .... in Aylesbury.
- **f** The groom throws food on the ....
- **g** The horses want to get away from the ....
- **h** James puts a .... round Black Beauty's head.
- **i** James runs into the .... again.
- **j** Joe Green cleans the ....

After you read

9 Work with another student. Have this conversation.

Student A: You are John Manly, the head groom. You want Joe Green to do James's job.

Student B: You are James Howard. You think Joe is too young for your job.

Chapters 9–11

Before you read

10 Discuss these questions. What do you think?

- **a** Black Beauty is going to leave Birtwick Park. Why?
- **b** Black Beauty's new home is at the country house of a very rich man, Lord Westland. In what ways will his life be different there?

While you read

11 Use the best question-word for these questions before you read these chapters. Then answer the questions while you read.

What Who Why

- **a** .... does John give a letter to at three o'clock in the morning?
  ....
- **b** .... will the doctor not want a whip?
  ....
- **c** .... is Black Beauty very ill after the ride from the doctor's house?
  ....
- **d** .... does John Manly want to do after he leaves Birtwick Park?
  ....
- **e** .... wants to put a bearing rein on Black Beauty?
  ....
- **f** .... does a bearing rein do?
  ....

After you read

12 Who are these people?

- **a** He lives in Hertford.
- **b** She is very ill.
- **c** He gives Black Beauty cold water.
- **d** His house is Earls Hall.
- **e** He is the boss of the drivers and the grooms.
- **f** She wants the horses' heads up.

13 What work do horses do in your country? Do you think people are unkind to horses today? In what ways? Talk about this with another student.

Chapters 12–15

Before you read

14 We meet Reuben Smith. He is a good driver and a good groom, but he isn't a good boss. Why, do you think? Talk about the ideas below with another student.

- **a** He doesn't like horses.
- **b** Horses don't like him.
- **c** He is very stupid.
- **d** He drinks too much.
- **e** Lord Westland doesn't like him.
- **f** He is always angry.
- **g** He says bad things to Lady Westland.

While you read

15 Are these sentences right (✓) or wrong (✗) ?

- **a** York doesn't like bearing reins. .....
- **b** Lord Westland sells Ginger after she falls. .....
- **c** Reuben Smith rides Black Beauty to Hertford. .....
- **d** Black Beauty falls on the road home. .....
- **e** Lord Westland sends Black Beauty to Hampstead. .....
- **f** A man buys Black Beauty for twenty-three pounds. .....
- **g** Jerry Barker has two children. .....
- **h** Black Beauty gets a new name. .....

After you read

16 Think about the work of horses in Black Beauty's time – on farms, in towns and cities and for sport. What kind of work was better or worse? Discuss this with another student.

Chapters 16–18

Before you read

17 In what ways do you think Black Beauty's life as a London cab horse will be different from his life before? What new things will he see? What new work will he do? Discuss this with another student.

18 Black Beauty is not a young horse now. Do you think his story will have a happy or a sad end?

While you read

19 Which of these things happen in these three chapters? Tick (✓) them.

a Black Beauty meets Ginger again. .....
b Jerry drives faster when people give him more money. .....
c Jerry and Black Beauty take a little boy to hospital. .....
d They take Mrs Barker to Paddington Station. .....
e Jerry gets very ill and dies. .....
f Mr Thoroughgood buys Black Beauty. .....
g Black Beauty meets Joe Green again. .....

After you read

20 'Today we don't use horses – we use cars. This is better, because people can't hurt cars.' What do you think of this idea?

21 Work with another student. Have this conversation.

Student A: You are Anna Sewell. You want to write a book about horses. Tell a friend why.

Student B: You are a friend of Anna Sewell. Why does she want to write this book? Ask her questions.

Writing

22 You are a horse today. What kind of work do you do? Who do you meet? Where do you live? Write about a day in your life.

23 You are living at the time of Black Beauty. You want to make things better for horses. Write a letter to a newspaper. What do you want to change?

24 Write a letter about *Black Beauty* to a friend. Did you enjoy the book? Write about the story. What did you like? What did you not like?

25 Write the story of Black Beauty in the fire (Chapter 7) in your words. What happened?

26 Think about the lives of Black Beauty and Ginger. In what ways were they the same or different? How did the two horses think or do things in different ways? Write about them.

27 Which person in the story do you like best? Which person do you not like? Why? Write about them.

28 Do you like horses? Can you ride a horse? Do you like dogs or cats more? Which animal do you like best? Write about it.

29 Do you think men or women like this story more? Write about this and say why.